What Readers Are
Every Man, God's Man
by Stephen Arterburn and Kenny Luck with Mike Yorkey

"Stephen Arterburn and Kenny Luck have captured the bold message men want and need to hear today. *Every Man, God's Man* speaks the language of men, urging them toward a new dimension of authentic faith and revealing the key principles they need to be God's man in every area of their lives."

—FISHER DEBERRY, head football coach,

U.S. Air Force Academy

"Every Man, God's Man holds a life-changing message for men. I applaud Arterburn and Luck for their efforts to challenge men in their pursuit of God and living godly lives. Every man needs to read and apply these truths."

—DAN QUAYLE, former vice president and author

of *Standing Firm*

"I am convinced that our great God and Savior wants to accomplish tremendous revival through today's Christian men. However, a vast percentage of them experience continual defeat and lack of growth in their spiritual development. Stephen Arterburn and Kenny Luck identify many of the problem areas men struggle with and how they can align themselves with God's purposes, becoming the spiritual victors and leaders He intended them to be."

—BILL BRIGHT, founder of Campus Crusade

for Christ International

"I have high regard for Stephen Arterburn and Kenny Luck and their positive message to men. Every man who wants to become all God created him to be will benefit from Steve and Kenny's counsel."

—JOSH MCDOWELL, best-selling author and speaker

every man, God's man

Pursuing Courageous Faith and Daily Integrity

workbook

Stephen Arterburn
Kenny Luck with Mike Yorkey

WATERBROOK
PRESS

EVERY MAN, GOD'S MAN WORKBOOK
PUBLISHED BY WATERBROOK PRESS
2375 Telstar Drive, Suite 160
Colorado Springs, Colorado 80920
A division of Random House, Inc.

Quotations from *Every Man, God's Man* © 2003 by Kenny Luck, Stephen Arterburn,
and Mike Yorkey.

All Scripture quotations, unless otherwise indicated, are taken from the *Holy Bible, New International Version*®. NIV®. Copyright © 1973, 1978, 1984 by International Bible Society. Used by permission of Zondervan Publishing House. All rights reserved. Scripture quotations marked (KJV) are taken from the *King James Version*.

Italics in Scripture quotations reflect the authors' added emphasis.

Details in some anecdotes and stories have been changed to protect the identities
of the persons involved.

ISBN 1-57856-691-6

Published in association with the literary agency of Alive Communications, Inc.,
7680 Goddard Street, Suite 200, Colorado Springs, Colorado 80920.

Printed in the United States of America
2003—First Edition

10 9 8 7 6 5 4 3 2 1

contents

questions you may have about this workbook

What will the *Every Man, God's Man Workbook* do for me?
Are you making progress where it counts? Are you dealing with the same character issues or fighting the same battles you fought a year ago? Are your relationships improving? Are you closing the gap between what you believe and how you really live? Many Christian men are discouraged by their honest answers to these questions. But there is hope: God has a plan to help His men complete the personal drive toward spiritual maturity and genuine manhood.

Part of the acclaimed Every Man series by popular counselor and speaker Stephen Arterburn, this workbook is specially designed to help today's Christian man personalize and apply the groundbreaking principles revealed in the best-selling book, *Every Man, God's Man.* Participants will be encouraged to evaluate where they are in their spiritual journeys; to become more intimate with God and truly give Him every area of their lives; and to live lives of lasting quality, purpose, and integrity.

Will this workbook be enough, or will I also need the book *Every Man, God's Man?*
Included in each weekly study you'll find a number of excerpts from the book *Every Man, God's Man,* each one marked at the beginning and end by

this symbol: 📖. Nevertheless, your best approach is to also read the book *Every Man, God's Man* as you go through this companion workbook. You'll find the appropriate chapters to read listed at the beginning of each weekly study.

The lessons look long. Do I need to work through all of each one?
This workbook is designed to promote your thorough exploration of all the material, but you may find it best to focus your time and discussion on some sections and questions more than others.

To help your pacing, we've designed the workbook so it can most easily be used in either an eight-week or twelve-week approach.

- *For the eight-week track,* simply *follow* along with the basic organization already set up with the eight different weekly lessons.
- *For the twelve-week track,* the *lessons* marked for weeks 2, 5, 6, and 7 can be divided into two parts (you'll see the dividing place marked in the text).

(In addition, of course, you may decide to follow at an even slower pace, whether you're going through the workbook by yourself or with a group.)

Above all, keep in mind that the purpose of the workbook is to help guide you in specific life-applications of the biblical truths taught in *Every Man, God's Man.* The wide variety of questions included in each weekly study is meant to help you approach this practical application from different angles and with personal reflection and self-examination. Allowing adequate time to prayerfully reflect on each question will be much more valuable to you than rushing through this workbook.

How do I bring together a small group to go through this workbook?
You'll get far more out of this workbook if you're able to go through it with a small group of like-minded men. And what do you do if you don't

know of a group that's going through the workbook? Start a group of your own!

If you show the book *Every Man, God's Man* and a copy of this companion workbook to Christian men you know, you'll be surprised at how many may indicate their interest in joining you to explore this topic together. And it doesn't require a long commitment. The workbook is clearly set up so you can complete one lesson per week and finish in only eight weeks—or if you'd like to proceed at a slower pace, you can follow the instructions provided for covering the content in a twelve-week track.

Your once-per-week meeting could happen during lunch hour at work, in the early morning before work begins, on a weekday evening, or even on a Saturday morning. The location could be an office or meeting room at work, a room at a club or restaurant, a classroom at church, or someone's basement or den at home. Choose a location where your discussion won't be overheard by others, so the men are comfortable in sharing candidly and freely.

This workbook follows a simple design that's easy to use. First, each man in the group completes a week's lesson on his own. Then, when you come together that week, you discuss together the group questions provided under the "Every Man's TALK" heading. Of course, if you have time, you can also discuss at length any of the other questions or topics in that week's lesson; we guarantee the men in your group will find these worth exploring. They're also likely to have plenty of their own related questions for discussion.

It's best if one person is designated as the group's facilitator. This person is not a lecturer or teacher but simply has the responsibility to keep the discussion moving and to ensure that each man in the group has an opportunity to fully join in.

At the beginning, and several times throughout the course, remind the men of the simple ground rule that *anything shared in the group stays in the group*—everything's confidential, especially considering the sensitive topics addressed in this study. This will help participants feel safer about sharing honestly and openly in an environment of trust.

Finally, we encourage you to allow time for prayer in each meeting—conversational, short-sentence prayers expressed in honesty before God. Be sensitive to the fact that many men don't feel comfortable praying aloud in front of others; over time, in an understanding way and without pressure, you can encourage them to overcome this barrier and participate aloud with the others.

All of this man-to-man experience has convinced me that far too many men do not give themselves fully to being God's man. It's like going three-and-out in a football game; they make three lackluster attempts to run or pass the ball, then they punt away their opportunity.

I want you to get back into the game and advance the ball downfield, pierce the red zone and ram it home, and enjoy greater intimacy with God as you connect with His plan and purposes for your future. God's goal is to finish the work in you—to have you stride into the end zone, legs kicking high—"that he who began a good work in you will carry it on to completion until the day of Christ Jesus" (Philippians 1:6).

—from Kenny Luck in chapter 1
of *Every Man, God's Man*

where are you
on this field?

This week's reading assignment:

the introduction and chapter 1 in *Every Man, God's Man*

So here's the bottom line of this book: The men's movement of the last fifteen years has been challenging men to love more, say more, pray more, read the Bible more, discipline themselves more, love their wives more, and serve their kids more. Men have wanted all those things, but the majority of them are failing over the long haul. The men's movement has asked men to do what their hearts and characters cannot deliver. Author Dallas Willard got it right: What's needed is a renovation of the heart before a renovation of lifestyle.

—from chapter 1 in *Every Man, God's Man*

EVERY MAN'S TRUTH
(Your Personal Journey into God's Word)

As you begin this study about becoming God's man, take some time to pray that God will do a work of transformation in your heart. Then delve into the Bible passages below, which talk about what it means to have the "heart renovation" the authors refer to in chapter 1. Don't rush into your study before carefully considering the state of your own heart in light of God's Word.

> Let not my heart be drawn to what is evil,
>> to take part in wicked deeds
> with men who are evildoers;
>> let me not eat of their delicacies.
>
> Let a righteous man strike me—it is a kindness;
>> let him rebuke me—it is oil on my head.
>> My head will not refuse it.
>
> Yet my prayer is ever against the deeds of evildoers;
>> their rulers will be thrown down from the cliffs,
>> and the wicked will learn that my words were well spoken.
> They will say, "As one plows and breaks up the earth,
>> so our bones have been scattered at the mouth of the
>>> grave. "
>
> But my eyes are fixed on you, O Sovereign LORD;
>> in you I take refuge—do not give me over to death.
> Keep me from the snares they have laid for me,
>> from the traps set by evildoers.
> Let the wicked fall into their own nets,
>> while I pass by in safety. (Psalm 141:4-10)
>
> Jesus called the crowd to him and said, "Listen and under-
> stand. What goes into a man's mouth does not make him
> 'unclean,' but what comes out of his mouth, that is what
> makes him 'unclean.'...

"Don't you see that whatever enters the mouth goes into the stomach and then out of the body? But the things that come out of the mouth come from the heart, and these make a man 'unclean.' For out of the heart come evil thoughts, murder, adultery, sexual immorality, theft, false testimony, slander. These are what make a man 'unclean'; but eating with unwashed hands does not make him 'unclean.'" (Matthew 15:10-11,17-20)

I keep asking that the God of our Lord Jesus Christ, the glorious Father, may give you the Spirit of wisdom and revelation, so that you may know him better. I pray also that the eyes of your heart may be enlightened in order that you may know the hope to which he has called you, the riches of his glorious inheritance in the saints, and his incomparably great power for us who believe. (Ephesians 1:17-19)

1. The psalmist prays that his heart will not be drawn to evil. In what situations is your own heart drawn most powerfully toward the wrong things?

2. Jesus cuts to the heart of our problems with sin. How would you apply this passage to your life right now? What personal heart problems are you aware of?

3. The apostle Paul prayed for the Ephesian believers. List the things he desired to see happening in their spiritual growth. Which one of these do you most desire in your own life?

4. What do you think Paul meant by enlightening "the eyes of your heart"?

☑ EVERY MAN'S CHOICE
(Questions for Personal Reflection and Examination)

📖 *Steve:* Please forgive me if you expect this book to start off with a super-stud football story or some other macho-inspired anecdote as men's books are supposed to do. In fact, I'm going to do a "Wrong Way Riegels" and run in the opposite direction by sharing a shameful antifootball story that happened to me. 📖

📖 *Steve:* We spend our lives doing stupid stuff to try to fit in, prove ourselves in the heat of battle, or show off our abilities. Our focus is on what other guys think, whoever they are. My contention is that we are playing to the wrong audience. God Almighty is the only audience we need. 📖

📖 *Kenny:* I wasn't being God's man. Under the blitz of financial pressure, my drive toward victory in Christ's kingdom stalled. At a time in my life when I should have been chewing up serious yards of turf in my service to Him, I bogged down in a financial quagmire and fumbled the ball. 📖

5. Do you have any "shameful" anti-stud incidents in your past? In what helpful or self-destructive ways have you learned to cope with such so-called failures of skill or nerve?

6. What things are you doing these days just to feel as if you fit in? How is this an attempt to play to the wrong audience?

7. Do you agree with the author that, like him, men are often "blitzed" by life and tend to fumble? If so, what are the primary areas of your life in which this tends to happen?

 EVERY MAN'S WALK
(Your Guide to Personal Application)

> 📖 *Steve:* Discovering the character of a godly man is what *Every Man, God's Man* is about. Isn't that what you really want? Don't you really want to do something that will grow you closer to God? As you read on, I want to give you a little guide that I call the Three Rs of God's man: Read, Recommit, and Relate. 📖

> 📖 *Kenny:* That day, the last major bastion of control fell into God's hands, and His victory was both humbling and liberating. Although I was awash in debt, I became the richest of all men because, deep inside, I was committed to the course. 📖

8. Do a personal self-evaluation according to the Three Rs of godly character development. How do you rate?

9. Why is it so hard for men to give up control to God? In what area of your life is this most difficult for you at the moment?

10. Kenny says, "You don't want to be in a hurry-up offense when you're in the red zone." Is rushing a problem for you? What specific activities could you let go of to make your daily routine a little less hectic (and give yourself some time for the Three Rs)?

11. Thoughtfully review the sixteen bulleted points at the end of chapter 1 that outline the themes to come in *Every Man, God's Man*. As of today, which of these topics do you think could have the most impact on your spiritual life as you proceed with your study?

12. In quietness, review what you have written and learned in this week's study. If further thoughts or prayer requests come to your mind and heart, you may want to write them here.

13. What for you was the most meaningful concept or truth in this week's study? What do you believe God wants you to do in response to this week's study?

How would you talk this over with God? Write your response here as a prayer to Him.

👥 EVERY MAN'S TALK

(Constructive Questions for Group Discussion)

Key Highlights from the Book to Read Aloud and Discuss

📖 *Steve:* My story begins on a dusty, hardscrabble high school football field in Bryan, Texas, where I hated almost every sweat-producing minute of every bone-crunching practice, none of which produced victories, because our sorry team lost nearly every game. I can still taste the dirt in my mouth from that grassless practice field. I can still feel my heaving breaths under thirty pounds of equipment, a flannel practice jersey, and humidity so thick that it cut the oxygen content by 50 percent.

Yes, you heard me right. I hated playing football. 📖

📖 *Steve:* Underneath all of your horrible habits or terrible treatment of others, you will find muscles of character. That character has been covered up by things of this world. Unless you are the reincarnation of Ted Bundy (the serial killer you will learn more about in chapter 11), the power of God can build on your character and help you become God's man, no matter what you have done or have been through. 📖

📖 *Kenny:* During the past several years, I have witnessed men commit to becoming God's man.… I've found that it's not about asking guys to *do* more; it's about asking them to *be* more. 📖

Discussion Questions

An opening question: Which parts of the introduction and chapter 1 were most helpful or encouraging to you? Why?

A. At the beginning of your time together, give everybody a chance to tell football stories. Men can talk about: (1) when they *played* the game, (2) when they *watched* a great game, or (3) why they never played and/or didn't *want* to.

B. What did you think about Steve's story of his football career (told in the introduction)? Who can relate from a sports point of view? Who can relate to the spiritual principles conveyed here?

C. Tell about how happy or discouraged you are with the state of your ab muscles these days. Talk about both your physical and spiritual musculature. Also comment on how the middle quote on the previous page lends some encouragement to you as you begin this study course.

D. Do you agree with Kenny's point that becoming God's man is more about being than doing? Why or why not? If there's time, spend some minutes going through the doing-being couplets that appear at the beginning of chapter 1. Ask for comments about how these principles have been realized in real life.

E. Kenny asks: "What bastions are you erecting against God's goodness and blessing in your life?" Take turns answering!

F. Talk about the relevance and application of Philippians 1:6 to the theme of this book—and to your own desire to grow as God's man.

G. Quickly review the bulleted outline of coming themes at the end of chapter 1. Ask each man to comment about which topics "ring a bell" with him at this point in his spiritual journey.

choosing to be God's man?

This week's reading assignment:

chapters 2–4 in *Every Man, God's Man*

With no duplicity, [God's man] has no hangovers of character. When he's away on business, he is the same person as he is at home. He is the same man on Friday and Saturday nights as he is on Sunday mornings. He's a father who says what he does and does what he says. He is a husband his wife can trust and follow.

God's man has moved beyond the payoff of instant gratification. Imagine it! Feeling good is replaced with feeling right about yourself.

—from chapter 2 in *Every Man, God's Man*

EVERY MAN'S TRUTH
(Your Personal Journey into God's Word)

Read and meditate on the Bible passages below before you begin this second study. You already know that making tough choices and properly ordering your priorities is a daily challenge. These verses can help strengthen your commitment in these areas. Let the Lord encourage you to hang tough!

I waited patiently for the LORD;
  he turned to me and heard my cry.
He lifted me out of the slimy pit,
  out of the mud and mire;
he set my feet on a rock
  and gave me a firm place to stand.
He put a new song in my mouth,
  a hymn of praise to our God.
Many will see and fear
  and put their trust in the LORD.

Blessed is the man
  who makes the LORD his trust,
who does not look to the proud,
  to those who turn aside to false gods.
Many, O LORD my God,
  are the wonders you have done.
The things you planned for us
  no one can recount to you;
were I to speak and tell of them,
  they would be too many to declare.

Sacrifice and offering you did not desire,
  but my ears you have pierced;
burnt offerings and sin offerings
  you did not require.
Then I said, "Here I am, I have come—
  it is written about me in the scroll.
I desire to do your will, O my God;
  your law is within my heart." (Psalm 40:1-8)

Do not store up for yourselves treasures on earth, where moth and rust destroy, and where thieves break in and steal. But store up for yourselves treasures in heaven, where moth and rust do not destroy, and where thieves do not break in and steal. For where your treasure is, there your heart will be also. (Matthew 6:19-21)

I do not understand what I do. For what I want to do I do not do, but what I hate I do. And if I do what I do not want to do, I agree that the law is good. As it is, it is no longer I myself who do it, but it is sin living in me. I know that nothing good lives in me, that is, in my sinful nature. For I have the desire to do what is good, but I cannot carry it out. For what I do is not the good I want to do; no, the evil I do not want to do—this I keep on doing. Now if I do what I do not want to do, it is no longer I who do it, but it is sin living in me that does it.

So I find this law at work: When I want to do good, evil is right there with me.... What a wretched man I am! Who will rescue me from this body of death? (Romans 7:15-21,24)

1. What words and phrases from Psalm 40 could you sincerely echo in a prayer to God right now? (Do it!)

2. What kinds of choices and priorities are called for, both in the psalm and in the words of Jesus?

3. To what extent can you relate to the apostle Paul's struggle to make the right choices in his life? What encouragement do you gain from Paul's honest confessions?

4. The apostle answered his own question (which he raised in Romans 7:24). Take a few minutes to read his thoughts on spiritual victory in Romans 8:1-17.

☑ EVERY MAN'S CHOICE

(Questions for Personal Reflection and Examination, Chapters 2 and 3)

> 📖 Mufasa nails the general feeling that grinds away at most Christian men: We are more than what we have become. We, too, are caught between divided loyalties and competing identities—real ones and false ones—which cause conflicting

angst. Like Simba, our time for talking has passed because
God is finished listening to the reasons why we can't move
forward. Our divided hearts must be confronted. 📖

📖 Spiritual integrity in the moment is an extension and
reflection of your true heart commitment. 📖

5. Think about Mufasa and Simba, then take some time to reflect upon
your identity. What is your real identity? What less-real identities do
you have?

6. The second quotation above states a key principle in *Every Man, God's
Man*. When have you seen this principle in action in your own life?

7. At the beginning of chapter 3, Kenny talks about an "erosion of character that is failing to stop the landslides of failure." Where are the
most seriously eroded places in your life's landscape?

8. Have you ever had a complete landslide of moral failure (or known another guy who did)? What have you learned from that situation?

👟 EVERY MAN'S WALK

(Your Guide to Personal Application, Chapters 2 and 3)

📖 In the first book of Chronicles, Israel's most proven veteran, a man named David, said, "I know, my God, that you test the heart and are pleased with integrity" (29:17). God will put our spiritual commitment into play over and over to reveal what's there. He will test it by giving us real-life opportunities to develop a practical consistency, and when we choose Him, He is pleased. *The goal is to choose God consistently under pressure and thereby develop spiritual integrity.* 📖

📖 As history has shown, God will give a man a desert experience to prepare him for the future.

Such a desert experience happened to my brother Chris. I'll never forget the late-night phone call from a frantic lady in Arizona. 📖

9. How good are you at interpreting tough times, or times of testing, as opportunities given to you by God? What is your typical reaction under this kind of pressure?

10. When was your last desert experience? Review the story of Chris and his desert period. What key insight do you gain from his remarkable renewal? How does his story apply to your story today?

11. Reread the last section of chapter 3, under "Creating that Inner Transformation." Recall how, in the Old Testament, Jacob confessed his character problem (his name) after wrestling with God. What would it take for you to candidly confess your character problems to God and another man? What would be the positive results from doing so?

12. In quietness, review what you have written and learned in this week's study. If further thoughts or prayer requests come to your mind and heart, you may want to write them here.

EVERY MAN'S TALK

(Constructive Questions for Group Discussion, Chapters 2 and 3)

Key Highlights from the Book to Read Aloud and Discuss

 📖 Intuitively, we know that to perform anything at a world-class level means that we cannot have a divided-heart commitment. And yet...many men, who understand what it takes to succeed in sport or business or the arts, are perfectly content to go through life with diluted or marginal spiritual outcomes. Why? Because of fear.

Afraid to pay the price in their commitment to Christ, men tend to consign themselves to some pseudo-identity absent His real influence. Half-cocked, lukewarm, and without a full identification in Christ, these men get what they get out of their relationship with God. 📖

📖 You are not alone when you admit that you have something less than sexual integrity.

Derek, for example, knew God's standard, but he began to entertain a lie regarding his relationships with women other than his wife. It wasn't what he did at first. It was what he *allowed*. Derek allowed himself to cultivate close friendships with female coworkers. 📖

📖 Once a man has given his life to Christ, God's aim is not to make him comfortable with the character and mannerisms that were ingrained into his psyche prior to becoming a member of the team. In fact, God's plan is for His Holy Spirit to bring about the necessary changes (although for stubborn characters and certain behavior patterns, His method of choice is to allow delays and difficulties to enter our lives). Character is carved out rather than instantly created. 📖

Discussion Questions for Chapters 2 and 3

An opening question: Which parts of chapters 2 and 3 were most helpful or encouraging to you? Why?

A. Begin your discussion time by talking briefly about the movie *The Lion King*. Invite any men who have seen it to give a brief movie-critic review, stating how many stars they would give this film and *why*.

B. Consider the authors' statement about the fear of "paying the price." Talk together about the other kinds of price mentioned. Who has paid that price to succeed in various arenas of achievement? Discuss what it takes—and why it seems so difficult—to apply the same energy to spiritual growth.

C. Together, review the story of Derek at the beginning of chapter 3. What was Derek's major mistake? Where do *you* set the boundaries in your relationships with females at work and elsewhere?

D. What does it mean that character must be carved out? What personal experiences prove this point?

E. Read the story of Jacob's wrestling match in Genesis 32:24-32. How do you apply this story to your own struggles to be God's man? What role has confessing your character problems (as Jacob did) played so far? What role can it play in the future?

Note: If you're following a twelve-week track,
save the rest of this lesson for the next session.
If you are on an eight-week track, keep going.

☑ EVERY MAN'S CHOICE
(Questions for Personal Reflection and Examination, Chapter 4)

📖 Maybe you haven't stooped as low as conning your four-year-old daughter out of a Pop-Tart, but we've all mentally rationalized doing the wrong thing over the years. Here are some of my all-time favorite justifications... 📖

📖 When Jesus Christ knocks at the door, He finds two types of men. One man runs. The other man opens the door. One man's commitment is insincere. The other man is eager to go to work with God. One man fears his charade will be exposed. The other man sees himself as a work in progress. One man knows that he habitually lies to himself. The other man works with God to deal with his shortcomings. One man makes himself scarce so no one will see who he really is. The other man allows others to see his progress. One man pretends to know God. The other man partners with God and gives Him credit for the good work that the truth accomplishes in his life. 📖

13. Look over the all-time favorites listed as rationalizations for doing wrong. Which ones do you most identify with? Why?

14. Of the two kinds of men, which are you at the moment? What is your specific evidence?

15. Kenny speaks of God's "weaving a tapestry" to help us overcome our fears of commitment. Do you agree with this word picture? Where do you see this phenomenon occurring in your own life?

 EVERY MAN'S WALK

(Your Guide to Personal Application, Chapter 4)

    ▣ What is Patrick going to say to the Lord, who knows all our thoughts? There are basically two ways to go, and we men tend to choose one or the other: We either face up to the truth, or we choose to run from it. ▣

    ▣ Other men I minister to are afraid to get honest because they find it too difficult to face their faults; after all, the cost of owning up to them is shame. ▣

16. Review the story of Patrick, the man who wanted to be a highway patrolman. If you had been his best friend while he was contemplating an affair, what would you have said and done to help him?

17. How difficult is it for you to face your faults? How have you avoided doing so in the past? What forms of shame have been involved?

18. Do you agree that facing up to the truth always involves some kind of loss? Why or why not? Tally some of the losses you are willing to experience in order to be God's man. Is becoming God's man worth those losses? Why or why not?

19. Prayerfully ask yourself the four bulleted questions that appear toward the end of chapter 4. (Don't rush this; ask God to be with you as you reveal your desire to connect more deeply with Him.)

20. What was the most meaningful concept or truth for you in this week's study? What action step or commitment do you believe God wants you to make in response? How would you talk this over with God? Write your response here as a prayer to Him.

EVERY MAN'S TALK

(Constructive Questions for Group Discussion, Chapter 4)

Key Highlights from the Book to Read Aloud and Discuss

A closer inspection revealed a blueberry Pop-Tart fresh from the toaster. I wanted one, too, but when I went to the cupboard, I discovered that the last pair of Pop-Tarts was sitting on my princess's plate. Without hesitation, I approached Jenna and informed her with a soft, loving voice that the second Pop-Tart on her plate had something yucky on it, and that I really needed to give it a taste test.

A man approached me once and asked if we could speak in private. This was his question: "If a person addicted to pornography has repented and stopped his habit for a month, should that person tell his wife?"

For some men, it's not about losing their public image or facing up to their faults as much as it is a fear of having to experience more pain as they face the truth about themselves. This was certainly the case for Jim, who had known nothing but pain all his life. His father was an abusive, chronic alcoholic. As if that weren't enough, a close family member had molested Jim when he was a young boy.

Discussion Questions for Chapter 4

An opening question: Which parts of chapter 4 were most helpful or encouraging to you? Why?

F. Begin your session by looking at Kenny's Pop-Tart ploy. Give everyone a chance to share about any similar tactics they've employed in the past.

G. Review the conversation with the man who asked about his addiction to pornography. What did you find helpful about Kenny's responses? What did you find unhelpful? Why?

H. Talk about Jim's story. Why did he run? What brought him back? What does Jim's experience tell you about God's way of working with men?

I. Ben was shocked to see his young son emulating his bad behavior. Talk about the times you've seen your children picking up a questionable (or rotten!) behavior from you. What lesson does that hold for someone committed to being God's man?

J. Neal pursued a double life with God. Have you ever tried that? How well did it work? Talk about it!

enter the fight— fearlessly!

This week's reading assignment:

chapters 5–6 in *Every Man, God's Man*

In the realm where battles of faith rage, a man must seek [a] bold new way of deal- ing with the forces that would harm his walk with God. Capitulation only delays the inevitable. Real change begins with a new perspective toward spiritual battle. Instead of it being "out there" and for others, we've got to make it a personal spir- itual crusade. Specifically, this means destroying the idea that we can be God's man and simultaneously accommodate old ways of behavior patterned after the world.

—from chapter 6 in *Every Man, God's Man*

EVERY MAN'S TRUTH

(Your Personal Journey into God's Word)

As you begin this study, think about the role of fear in your life. Consider making a list of your top five fears and making this list a subject of daily prayer. Also, take encouragement from the Bible passages below. Realize that, as God's man, you can learn to face your fears rather than run from

them. The first step is simply acknowledging the things that scare you the
most. Are you ready to do that?

> The LORD is my light and my salvation—
> > whom shall I fear?
> The LORD is the stronghold of my life—
> > of whom shall I be afraid?
> When evil men advance against me
> > to devour my flesh,
> when my enemies and my foes attack me,
> > they will stumble and fall.
> Though an army besiege me,
> > my heart will not fear;
> though war break out against me,
> > even then will I be confident.
>
> One thing I ask of the LORD,
> > this is what I seek:
> that I may dwell in the house of the LORD
> > all the days of my life,
> to gaze upon the beauty of the LORD
> > and to seek him in his temple.
> For in the day of trouble
> > he will keep me safe in his dwelling;
> he will hide me in the shelter of his tabernacle
> > and set me high upon a rock.
> Then my head will be exalted
> > above the enemies who surround me;
> at his tabernacle will I sacrifice with shouts of joy;
> > I will sing and make music to the LORD. (Psalm 27:1-6)

Who shall separate us from the love of Christ? Shall trouble or hardship or persecution or famine or nakedness or danger or sword? As it is written:

"For your sake we face death all day long;
we are considered as sheep to be slaughtered."

No, in all these things we are more than conquerors through him who loved us. For I am convinced that neither death nor life, neither angels nor demons, neither the present nor the future, nor any powers, neither height nor depth, nor anything else in all creation, will be able to separate us from the love of God that is in Christ Jesus our Lord. (Romans 8:35-39)

For God hath not given us the spirit of fear; but of power, and of love, and of a sound mind. (2 Timothy 1:7, KJV)

1. What is the psalmist's most basic defense against all kinds of fear?

2. To what extent are you claiming this defense in your life? What first steps could you take to become more reliant on the stronghold of your life?

3. When have you most deeply known the love of God? Are you, too, convinced that nothing can separate you from this love? What types of situations most powerfully challenge this truth in your life?

4. Be Timothy for a moment. Take some time to savor the apostle Paul's encouraging words to you about fear.

☑ EVERY MAN'S CHOICE
(Questions for Personal Reflection and Examination)

📖 What I like…is the way Ryan gave up control and risked real trust. He could have kept resisting, and I could have insisted that they pull that tube from his nose and unstrap him. Neither action would have helped the situation, however. Instead, we had to believe in the wisdom and skill of our nurses and doctors.…

Many men I counsel are stuck with a hurt they can't get over, a habit they can't change, or other people who rob them of joy. Instead of trusting the One who can guide them safely out, they fight God—even though He's saying, "This may hurt a bit, but you're going to feel a whole lot better when it's over." 📖

📖 Professionally, [Danny's] pride had kept God out of the workplace. It's as if Danny had reserved control over a domain that he knew should belong to God. Whenever that happens, God has a way of showing us that we don't know as much as we think we do. He will act to show us that we do not know better than He does. 📖

📖 Before his departure, Jesus pulled His men in tight to tell them, "If you belonged to the world, it would love you as its own. As it is, you do not belong to the world, but I have chosen you out of the world. That is why the world hates you" (John 15:19). His message to them is the same for us: *Blending in with the world is not the mark of a follower of Christ.* 📖

5. Think about Ryan's giving up control to the doctors. How do you react to the idea of giving up control of your life to God? When have you tried to do that? What happened?

6. Like Danny, do you have parts of your life that you keep off-limits to God? What are they, and why do you think you resist giving Him control of these areas?

7. If you sense hatred or persecution coming toward you as a Christian at times, what is Jesus' explanation?

👟 EVERY MAN'S WALK
(Your Guide to Personal Application)

📖 I really thought a car loaded with sex appeal and that cornered well would fundamentally alter my identity and happiness....

If this is what the world is selling, then why are we buying? And I'm talking about more than goods and services. I'm talking about buying into the world's shortsighted value system, integrating its shallow thinking into our Christian walk.

I'm talking about blending in. 📖

📖 In other words, loving God means resisting the world moment by moment. It's putting forceful, compelling feelings aside in order to remain obedient. It's placing another person's need above our need to do something or be somewhere. It's choosing purity of mind and body and exercising spiritual discipline that honors God. It's saying no to impulses that place a higher priority on material things than on people. It's being real and honest rather than just preserving an image....

To gain Christ in our lives, we must lose the world. 📖

8. Think of two or three things you have bought in the past purely for the sex appeal. Are you still seeking to blend in by this method?

9. In the second quote above, which phrase stands out to you as being most applicable to your life? How will you let this idea move you to resist the world today and tomorrow?

10. Read and meditate on Luke 9:24-25 (quoted at the end of chapter 6). How do Jesus' words directly counter the myth of coexistence? How, specifically, do you envision applying His words in the days ahead?

11. In quietness, review what you have written and learned in this week's study. If further thoughts or prayer requests come to your mind and heart, you may want to write them here.

12. What for you was the most meaningful concept or truth in this week's study? What action step(s) do you believe God wants you to take in response?

How would you talk this over with God? Write your response here as a prayer to Him.

👥 EVERY MAN'S TALK
(Constructive Questions for Group Discussion)

Key Highlights from the Book to Read Aloud and Discuss

> 📖 Instead of trusting the One who can guide them safely out, they fight God—even though He's saying, "This may hurt a bit, but you're going to feel a whole lot better when it's over."
>
> "No thanks," we reply....
>
> Whether God is calling you to some great mission or simply moving you to confess a failing, the fear of the unknown may make you uncomfortable. Maybe it should. Your discomfort could be a sign of an inner war for control of your life. 📖

📖 A few days later, Tim was fired for stealing from the company—another example of someone who thought he had to take matters into his own hands because he was on his own. His fear that God wouldn't provide blinded him to the greatest promise of all: "Seek first his kingdom and his righteousness, and all these things will be given to you as well" (Matthew 6:33). Tim hedged his bet on God's promise and lost it all when he should have believed that God knew the best way to meet his needs. 📖

📖 All of us have heard the siren song of beliefs that suit our tastes, dispositions, politics, and lifestyles. In our culture we're free to believe what we want because, in the name of tolerance and diversity, no one's viewpoint can be dismissed. And while this might help us be liked by others and be viewed as broad-minded, it is a dangerous approach to take—like making a beeline for a deadly reef upon which we're likely to shipwreck our faith. 📖

Discussion Questions

An opening question: Which parts of chapters 5 and 6 were most helpful or encouraging to you? Why?

A. How is yielding to God's work like going to the dentist—something that "may hurt a bit"?

B. When have you had the greatest fear of the unknown? How did you cope?

C. Tim hedged his bets with God. When have you had the most fear that God wouldn't come through for you? Did you, like Tim, hedge your bet? What was the result?

D. What do you think of the appeal of being seen by society as broad-minded and tolerant these days? What are the dangers here?

E. Review the last section of chapter 6, "Ride the Pendulum Wisely." Have each man identify the issues in his life that cause him to swing the pendulum toward—or away from—God's way. Then pray for one another.

know your enemy

As I work with men, I have seen how giving up certain inner beachheads—spiritual footholds—determines our spiritual destinies time and time again. These footholds are the small but strategic areas of a man's life that either keep him under the rule of the world—the flesh and the devil—or liberate him spiritually to achieve the next level. Control of these beachheads is critical, which is why the Bible warns us: "Do not give the devil a foothold" (Ephesians 4:27).

—from chapter 8 in *Every Man, God's Man*

📖 EVERY MAN'S TRUTH
(Your Personal Journey into God's Word)

Warfare. It's not reserved just for battlefields between nations. No, according to this week's readings in *Every Man, God's Man*, we are involved in a daily battle with the forces of spiritual darkness. Will we fight well? Will we win?

Let your heart be encouraged by the scriptures below as you enter the daily fray. Yes, you have already won the war, through your Savior's heroic sacrifice. Now He gives you every piece of equipment you need to make that victory sure and practical in your daily life. Read all about it…

Now if we died with Christ, we believe that we will also live with him. For we know that since Christ was raised from the dead, he cannot die again; death no longer has mastery over him. The death he died, he died to sin once for all; but the life he lives, he lives to God.

In the same way, count yourselves dead to sin but alive to God in Christ Jesus. Therefore do not let sin reign in your mortal body so that you obey its evil desires. Do not offer the parts of your body to sin, as instruments of wickedness, but rather offer yourselves to God, as those who have been brought from death to life; and offer the parts of your body to him as instruments of righteousness. For sin shall not be your master, because you are not under law, but under grace....

You have been set free from sin and have become slaves to righteousness. (Romans 6:8-14,18)

Be strong in the Lord and in his mighty power. Put on the full armor of God so that you can take your stand against the devil's schemes. For our struggle is not against flesh and blood, but against the rulers, against the authorities, against the powers of this dark world and against the spiritual forces of evil in the heavenly realms. Therefore put on the full armor of God, so that when the day of evil comes, you may be able to stand your ground, and after you have done everything, to stand. Stand firm then, with the belt of truth buckled around your waist, with the breastplate of righteousness in place, and with your feet fitted with the readiness that comes from the gospel of peace. In addition to all this, take up the shield of faith, with which you can extinguish all the flaming arrows of the evil one. Take the helmet of salvation and the sword of the Spirit, which is the word of God. And pray in the Spirit on all occasions with all kinds of prayers and requests. With this in mind, be alert and always keep on praying for all the saints. (Ephesians 6:10-18)

Grace and peace be yours in abundance through the knowledge of God and of Jesus our Lord.

His divine power has given us everything we need for life and godliness through our knowledge of him who called us by his own glory and goodness. Through these he has given us his very great and precious promises, so that through them you may participate in the divine nature and escape the corruption in the world caused by evil desires. (2 Peter 1:2-4)

1. What does it mean to you, in practical terms, to live under grace rather than under law? How did Christ's actions win this privilege for you?

2. Make a list of the pieces of armor God provides for spiritual warfare. Which do you still need to put on?

3. If you've been given everything you need for godliness, what is holding you back?

4. What does it mean to you to know that you may participate in the divine nature?

☑ EVERY MAN'S CHOICE
(Questions for Personal Reflection and Examination)

📖 Sometimes, in my journey with God, I feel as though there is a mole within me, lurking in my thoughts, dropping suggestions that run counter to God's plan. The Kenny Luck Mole transmits disinformation that confuses and contradicts the clear instruction of God's Word. My mole seizes my physical appetites and senses, encouraging indulgence when restraint would better serve my faith, my character, my family, and my friends. 📖

📖 The mole sets up an ambush by making the action he wants you to take appear justified, rational, righteous, deserving, logical, or pleasurable to get you to buy in. This ad campaign gets even tougher when you hear the culture saying things like "It's not going to hurt anyone," "You'll feel better after this," "No one will know," or "Just one more time." The mole knows how to tempt you because he *is* you—the old you. 📖

📖 For years Jeremy has allowed his eyes to feed on women's bodies. Jeremy is what alcoholics would call a sipper: He doesn't keep a stash of *Hustler* magazines in the basement, but he never stops his eyes from roaming when he's out and about. No bikini, no low-cut blouse, no sports bra, no bare midriff, and no tight buns escape his heat-seeking eyes....

Jeremy never anticipated someone ever looking back, but she did. 📖

5. What is your reaction to the idea of a personal "mole"? Do you have one? If so, how would you describe its tactics and actions in your life?

6. Think back over the last few months and consider: In what situations has your mole been the most active? Why do you think this has been happening? How have you responded?

7. In light of Jeremy's downfall, can you relate to his naiveté about the apparent harmlessness of looking? What is the real problem with being a "sipper"?

 EVERY MAN'S **WALK**

(Your Guide to Personal Application)

 📖 The first step to deflating the mole is knowing you have one and knowing its goal. Jesus identified it for us when He warned, "The spirit is willing but the flesh is weak." 📖

 📖 Speaking truth brings the mole out into the open.
 I've found that the only way for me to deal effectively with the mole's siren call is to come out swinging. I have to go into boxer mode and pepper my opponent with several jabs to keep him off balance. After I call him what he is, I *call out* Scripture audibly.
 That's God's calling plan. 📖

8. How are you planning to fight, on a daily basis, your "old man" or mole? What specific plans can you develop?

9. What does Kenny mean by the idea of coming out swinging? Do you think this approach would work for you? Why or why not?

10. Read Psalm 145:18-19. Then compose a brief "call out" prayer to use the next time your mole is tempting you.

11. Think about what it takes to win back a foothold by reviewing the overall advice given in chapter 8. What two or three ideas would you like to implement in your own spiritual warfare battle plans?

12. In quietness, review what you have written and learned in this week's study. If further thoughts or prayer requests come to your mind and heart, you may want to write them here.

13. What for you was the most meaningful concept or truth in this week's study? What action steps do you think God wants you to take in response?

How would you talk this over with God? Write your response here as a prayer to Him.

👨👨 EVERY MAN'S TALK
(Constructive Questions for Group Discussion)

Key Highlights from the Book to Read Aloud and Discuss

> 📖 It was early on a Saturday morning, but I already had my Starbucks grande vanilla latte in my right hand and that's all that mattered. Life was good as I relished each sip of my sweet, caffeinated concoction while en route to my daughter Cara's soccer game. 📖

> 📖 A friend told me that Alan was divorcing Karen. I immediately called Alan and asked if we could meet. When we did, the first words out of his mouth were, "I am not like you, Kenny." This was followed by, "You don't know the whole picture."

I nodded my head. "Really? Can I tell you what I do know, bro?" 📖

📖 It all began when [Jeremy] allowed a lovely woman to gain a foothold as she returned his long glance. You see, the only difference between spiritual warfare and actual warfare is the bloodletting. But lives still get destroyed anyway. 📖

Discussion Questions

An opening question: Which parts of chapters 7 and 8 were most helpful or encouraging to you. Why?

A. To open your session, spend some time talking about Kenny's Saturday-morning vanilla latte story near the start of chapter 7. Who can relate to the attitudes and feelings Kenny reveals? Who has a similar story to share?

B. Review the story of Alan and Karen in chapter 7. Do you think Kenny should have confronted Alan the way he did? (Support your response with scripture.) What was effective about the confrontation? How might you have done it differently?

C. Together, read back through the case of Jeremy in chapter 8. Then take plenty of time to analyze the eleven examples of footholds listed on page 101. Ask volunteers to comment on which ones seem to be a part of their own lives.

D. The authors state, "God's man speaks the scriptures into his daily challenges." Do you agree? If so, spend some time sharing favorite scripture passages that can be deployed in the battle against moles and devilish footholds. Jot down your favorites, encourage one another to commit them to memory, and use them this week!

E. Focus several minutes of your remaining time on the final section of chapter 8, "Winning Back Those Footholds." First, talk about the three ways to stand against the enemy. Then discuss Brett's decision to openly and honestly share his struggles with Internet porn. What risks did he face? What benefits did he gain?

F. Is your men's group a safe place for such sharing? Are you committed to honesty, confidentiality, accountability—and most important, to praying for one another? Talk about why you like meeting as a group and how the group might do better in these vital areas.

what does it take?

This week's reading assignment:

chapters 9–11 in *Every Man, God's Man*

Many men serve their own interests by having "a form of godliness but denying its power." For instance, men know when they are sexually violating God's law, but they continue to unzip their pants anyway. Husbands know when they are tearing down their spouses, but they continue the verbal tirades. Fathers know when their kids are just dying for some time with Dad, but they find other things to do anyway. In contrast, when God's man is tempted to enter 80/20 territory, he does what God would rather have him do—even if it's less convenient or not nearly as fun.

—from chapter 9 in *Every Man, God's Man*

📖 EVERY MAN'S TRUTH
(Your Personal Journey into God's Word)

You already know that becoming God's man calls for a radical character transformation. But it's a change of heart that begins with a change of mind. Read and meditate on the Bible passages below, which deal with this spiritual mind transformation. As you read and meditate, open yourself to the work of the Holy Spirit; invite Him to renew your mind so that it will become more and more like the mind of Christ.

I have hidden your word in my heart
   that I might not sin against you.
Praise be to you, O LORD;
   teach me your decrees.
With my lips I recount
   all the laws that come from your mouth.
I rejoice in following your statutes
   as one rejoices in great riches.
I meditate on your precepts
   and consider your ways.
I delight in your decrees;
   I will not neglect your word. (Psalm 119:11-16)

For though we live in the world, we do not wage war as the world does. The weapons we fight with are not the weapons of the world. On the contrary, they have divine power to demolish strongholds. We demolish arguments and every pretension that sets itself up against the knowledge of God, and we take captive every thought to make it obedient to Christ. (2 Corinthians 10:3-5)

Do not be anxious about anything, but in everything, by prayer and petition, with thanksgiving, present your requests to God. And the peace of God, which transcends all understanding, will guard your hearts and your minds in Christ Jesus.

Finally, brothers, whatever is true, whatever is noble, whatever is right, whatever is pure, whatever is lovely, whatever is admirable—if anything is excellent or praiseworthy—think about such things. Whatever you have learned or received or heard from me, or seen in me—put it into practice. And the God of peace will be with you. (Philippians 4:6-9)

1. In light of the three Bible passages above, what role does the mind play in character transformation?

2. What does it mean to delight in God's decrees? Where are you on the "delight scale" these days? Why are you at that particular point?

3. What kinds of thoughts would you like to take captive in the days ahead? What is your plan to demolish this mental stronghold?

4. Under the headings that Paul gives in Philippians 4, list some of the specific things you'd like to think more about in the days ahead. That is, what things are true, noble, right, and so on?

☑ EVERY MAN'S CHOICE

(Questions for Personal Reflection and Examination, Chapters 9 and 10)

📖 *Selective obedience to the will of God.* We hear what we want to hear, reject what's not in sync with our personal desires, replace God's instruction with our own whims, and act out our own plan when it works best for us. 📖

📖 If oil produces the lubrication necessary for engines to deliver the designed performance, then *humility* lubricates a man's faith, producing results in his spiritual life. The Bible teaches that humility is the one core attitude that God's man goes after as he seeks to make his relationship with the Lord work. 📖

5. From your reading of chapter 9, how would you define selective obedience? Can you recall a specific instance of this in your own life?

6. Why is humility so important to spiritual growth as God's man? (Suggestion: Why not take a moment to invite the Lord to bring more humility into your character?)

🥾 EVERY MAN'S WALK
(Your Guide to Personal Application, Chapters 9 and 10)

📖 Consider the cases of three guys who are following in Saul's footsteps, though perhaps in more subtle (though no less devastating) ways today. 📖

📖 Being God's man will never be easy, but those who have passed the test did so because they successfully overcame the opinions of others, successfully fought their own feelings and weaknesses of character, and successfully contended with spiritual opposition. Abraham of the Old Testament was God's man. 📖

7. Go back and reread the section subtitled "Succumbing to the 80/20 Syndrome" in chapter 9. As you review each of the three case studies, ask yourself: In what ways am I like or unlike this guy?

8. Consider your biblical role models mentioned in chapter 9 under "Following Our Ancient Mentors." Which do you most admire? Why? How are you hoping to follow in their footsteps?

9. Think about the story of the prodigal son as described in chapter 10. How does Jesus' story illustrate "Lord-love" for you? What truth stands out from the story about the heavenly Father's love for you?

10. In quietness, review what you have written and learned in this week's study. If further thoughts or prayer requests come to your mind and heart, you may want to write them here.

👀 EVERY MAN'S TALK

(Constructive Questions for Group Discussion, Chapter 9 and 10)

Key Highlights from the Book to Read Aloud and Discuss

📖 Every honest man knows the struggle and pain of selective obedience. On more than one occasion, King Saul of the

Old Testament could not resist his impulses to mess with God's clear instruction. He is a timeless poster child for every man arrogant enough to turn his back on God's revealed will. 📖

📖 Now let's switch gears and look at the case of a man who knows how to avoid the 80/20 syndrome. My friend Paul is an airline pilot with a major carrier. Paul tells me that every time he puts on his uniform, he is challenged as a Christian.

"You wouldn't believe what goes on during two- and three-day trips away from home," he tells me. 📖

📖 Humility doesn't save a man eternally, but it sure saves him a ton of grief. Humility doesn't change a man's circumstances, but it helps him see God's purposes. Humility doesn't speed up answers to prayer, but it accelerates acceptance of God's will. Humility doesn't make decisions for a man, but it weights his heart toward decisions consistent with God's plan. Humility doesn't earn a man more of God's love, but it helps him experience God's love at a deeper level. Scripture piles it on when it comes to the subject of humility. 📖

Discussion Questions for Chapters 9 and 10

An opening question: Which parts of chapters 9 and 10 were most helpful or encouraging to you? Why?

A. Begin by talking about the television show *Everybody Loves Raymond.* Get the guys' opinions on the show, and then talk about the specific episode described in the opening of chapter 9. Answer the mother's question: "Can you just pick and choose [from the Ten Commandments]?"

B. Review the ways King Saul practiced selective obedience in his life. What can we learn from his example?

C. Talk about Paul, the airline pilot, and the incredible temptations that came his way. How was he able to avoid the 80/20 syndrome?

D. In the third quotation on page 57, the authors make some claims for the benefits of humility. Go through each one together, and find out whether the guys in your group agree or disagree. Have them cite specific examples they may have observed in their own lives or in God's men around them.

E. How can you tell if you have significant humility in your character?

F. Focus attention on the final section of chapter 10, which deals with Collin's story. What does it take for today's man to "take the humble position" with a spouse or other loved one?

Note: If you're following a twelve-week track,
save the rest of this lesson for the next session.
If you are on an eight-week track, keep going.

☑ EVERY MAN'S CHOICE

(Questions for Personal Reflection and Examination, Chapter 11)

📖 In a sense, our male minds are like those pork ribs: They take on the character of whatever we soak them in. Only after going through the fire, however, does our true flavor come out. Allow me to illustrate this principle through two examples of two very different men. 📖

📖 So how does God's man marinate his mind in the precepts and ways of the Lord? The Bible gives us the principle of *meditation*, as we read in Psalm 119:23: "Your servant will meditate on your decrees."

The defining marker for God's man is that he thinks deeply and continuously about what God has spoken. 📖

11. In what are you soaking your mind? Name some of the ingredients of your mind's typical daily marinade. Anything in it that could be toxic?

12. What has been your experience with meditating on God's Word? After reading chapter 11, what new insights have you gained to help you in this vital area?

📓 EVERY MAN'S WALK

(Your Guide to Personal Application, Chapter 11)

📖 "Kenny, the temptation was too irresistible," Cameron said.

"What do you mean?" I inquired.

"I mean when I was alone with Mandy, it was like something else just took over. It was like I was helpless." 📖

📖 If you're the leader of a million people and you're trying to keep the whole deal together in addition to overtaking foreign lands occupied by people who don't like you, what would *you* say is the X-factor for success? God said it was to *think deeply and continuously on His Word* so that you will do what He says first. 📖

13. Do you agree that there is no such thing as an irresistible temptation? Why or why not? If indeed there is no such thing as an irresistible temptation, what kinds of things in your life need to be resisted right now?

14. The authors cite the example of the biblical Joshua. What was the key to Joshua's success? How is this encouraging to you?

15. The authors claim that spending time with God is more about set-
ting priorities than scheduling time. Do you find that you are making
Bible reading a priority these days? If not, what first step toward
change could you take?

16. What for you was the most meaningful concept or truth in this week's
study? What do you believe God wants you to do in response?

How would you talk this over with God? Write your response here as a
prayer to Him.

EVERY MAN'S TALK
(Constructive Questions for Group Discussion, Chapter 11)

Key Highlights from the Book to Read Aloud and Discuss

Two men, two marinades, two radically different legacies—but one unmistakable truth: The content of the mind
creates the character of a man. Think about it. Men who give

most of their mental energy to the next toy they're going to buy are materialists. A guy who's always maneuvering himself into opportunities to impress others can be classified as a narcissist—"a legend in his own mind." 📖

📖 One Thursday morning at our men's Bible study at church, I posed the following discussion question to Darren and others in the room: "What is keeping you *out* of God's Word? Or perhaps you can answer the opposite question: What is keeping you *in* God's word?"

Darren was first to jump in the water. "I've struggled for years with reading the Bible," he began. 📖

Discussion Questions for Chapter 11

An opening question: Which parts of chapter 11 were most helpful or encouraging to you? Why?

G. Chapter 11 begins with a full description of Kenny's famous pork ribs. Ask the guys in your group to tell about the favorite dishes that they like to eat or cook.

H. According to the principles in this chapter, why did the two men— Ted Bundy and Billy Graham—end up with such radically different legacies? What is the authors' main point in telling their stories?

I. Can you relate to Darren's struggles with reading the Bible? Talk about what helps and hinders this desire. (Refer to anything in Darren's experience that sheds light on the path to consistent reading.)

J. Do you agree that there is no such thing as an irresistible temptation? Why or why not? Think about some of the scenarios that we often dwell upon prior to a particularly tempting situation. How do these advance imaginings contribute to a guy's downfall?

K. Kenny often asks, "Where is your Tent of Meeting?" How would you answer?

L. Based on your study of chapter 11 of *Every Man, God's Man,* what specific action step do you sense God leading you to take, starting today? (Suggestion: Have the men in your group pray for one another as they identify and commit to whatever action steps or attitude change God is surfacing for them.)

close allies

This week's reading assignment:
chapters 12–14 in *Every Man, God's Man*

Close connections between God's men are fueling the next wave of spiritual revolution. We are discovering the life-changing difference such relationships can make, and we are becoming close allies in the battle to finish strong.

—from chapter 12 in *Every Man, God's Man*

EVERY MAN'S TRUTH
(Your Personal Journey into God's Word)

The great thing about pursuing growth in spiritual character is that we are not expected to go it alone. First, if we are willing to be open and confess our struggles, we can find encouragement and help through genuine fellowship with our brothers in Christ. Second, guidance and strength are available from the Spirit of God who dwells within us. This is crucial to know because any spiritual transformation we experience is not, ultimately, the result of our own efforts. Rather, it is the result of the Holy Spirit's gracious work within us as we allow Him control. The Bible passages below make clear just who the Holy Spirit is and what He wants to do in us. Let these truths sink into your heart as you prepare for this week's study.

I will ask the Father, and he will give you another Counselor to be with you forever—the Spirit of truth. The world cannot accept him, because it neither sees him nor knows him. But you know him, for he lives with you and will be in you. (John 14:16-17)

Those who live according to the sinful nature have their minds set on what that nature desires; but those who live in accordance with the Spirit have their minds set on what the Spirit desires. The mind of sinful man is death, but the mind controlled by the Spirit is life and peace; the sinful mind is hostile to God. It does not submit to God's law, nor can it do so. Those controlled by the sinful nature cannot please God.

You, however, are controlled not by the sinful nature but by the Spirit, if the Spirit of God lives in you. And if anyone does not have the Spirit of Christ, he does not belong to Christ. (Romans 8:5-9)

No one knows the thoughts of God except the Spirit of God. We have not received the spirit of the world but the Spirit who is from God, that we may understand what God has freely given us. This is what we speak, not in words taught us by human wisdom but in words taught by the Spirit, expressing spiritual truths in spiritual words. The man without the Spirit does not accept the things that come from the Spirit of God, for they are foolishness to him, and he cannot understand them, because they are spiritually discerned. The spiritual man makes judgments about all things, but he himself is not subject to any man's judgment:

"For who has known the mind of the Lord
that he may instruct him?"

But we have the mind of Christ. (1 Corinthians 2:11-16)

1. If the Holy Spirit is the Counselor living within you, how often during your typical day do you stop to listen to Him?

2. What is your mind set on today? According to Roman 8:5-9, how does that affect your desires?

3. According to 1 Corinthians 2:11-12, for what key reason have we received the Spirit?

4. What precious truths do you understand about the Lord because of the Spirit's ministry in you?

☑ EVERY MAN'S CHOICE
(Questions for Personal Reflection and Examination, Chapters 12 and 13)

📖 "Kenny, I was so alone."

In that moment, Hans defined what I believe is the number-one dilemma facing Christian men: isolation. Today, more than any other time in history, American men feel emotionally and relationally isolated. Sure, we have friends, and we are certainly leading busy lives. But as a general condition, we males are not connected to one another for any deep purposes. 📖

📖 Confession is about breaking the silence and risking being found out, as I discovered in a most personal way. This is very difficult because secrets are often the last domain of a man's control. On the flip side, bringing to light closely held secrets can be the most liberating, freeing, and transforming thing we will ever do. In fact, I would say it is impossible for God's man to confess until he can admit openly his defects, sins, and struggles to both God *and* man. 📖

5. Kenny believes the number-one dilemma facing men is isolation. Do you agree? Has this been true in your life? What do you do to cope?

6. Are you willing to risk being found out? What would it take for you to reveal a few closely held secrets to another guy?

7. Recall Kenny's comments about the emotional "Sweeper" early in chapter 13. What mistakes or emotions have you swept under the surface lately? Why?

🥾 EVERY MAN'S WALK
(Your Guide to Personal Application, Chapters 12 and 13)

> 📖 At every men's conference, I encounter God's men who confess to dabbling in Internet porn, illicit affairs, and way

too many substances. Others immerse themselves in their work, a sports team, or some hobby to help them deal with life's pain. Unfortunately, these diversions are exactly that— diversions. I have found that men who are not progressing personally, spiritually, or relationally have reached this sad state because they do not risk connecting on an honest level with other men. But we need to! Men relating to other men is right where God wants us to be. 📖

📖 I've found that men do not become men in the company of women. Please understand, I'm not dissing the ladies when I make this statement. It's simply the way God created us. *Men become men in the company of men.* Ask any warrior in any culture. 📖

8. Think about your favorite diversions from legitimate emotion. How do you tend to deal with life's pain?

9. Are you regularly involved in the company of men committed to encouraging and praying for one another? If not, what are your options for seeking a men's group?

10. In quietness, review what you have written and learned in this week's
    study. If further thoughts or prayer requests come to your mind and
    heart, you may want to write them here.

EVERY MAN'S TALK

(Constructive Questions for Group Discussion, Chapters 12 and 13)

Key Highlights from the Book to Read Aloud and Discuss

📖 Now I realize I'm talking about a Hollywood movie
[Cast Away]. But just as severed communication doomed
Chuck to being a lonely castaway, I have seen firsthand how
the lack of communication and connection among men has crea-
ted a culture of spiritual castaways. Pulled off course in their
walks with God, not reporting their spiritual or personal status to anyone, no one knows them or where they are with
the Lord. Their spiritual compasses are definitely off track.
Time passes, and when the typhoons of temptation strike,
they drift *way* off course. 📖

📖 Men relating to other men is right where God wants
us to be. It's where we can get help when we need it most,
watch each other's backs, pray for and encourage one
another, and care enough to confront so that we help
each other become the men God created us to be: "My
brothers, if one of you should wander from the truth and
someone should bring him back, remember this: Whoever

turns a sinner from the error of his way will save him
from death and cover over a multitude of sins"
(James 5:19-20). 📖

📖 When it comes to dealing with our emotions, men run
for the hills—alone. We are not good at facing our feelings,
let alone talking about them. Most of us have been trained to
treat our emotions like smelly socks that need to be washed,
dried, and put back in the drawer.

When emotions surface, the "Sweeper" moves in. 📖

Discussion Questions for Chapters 12 and 13

An opening question: Which parts of chapters 12 and 13 were most helpful
or encouraging to you? Why?

A. Begin your group time by talking about the movie *Cast Away.* Who
   has seen it? What did they think? Then move on to discuss the first
   quotation above. Consider: How important is it to report our personal
   and spiritual status to others? What are the benefits (and risks)? What
   has been your personal experience in mutual accountability with other
   like-minded men?

B. What does it mean to you to "care enough to confront"? Can you give
   a personal example of a time when you were either the giver or receiver
   of this kind of caring?

C. Why do we men tend to treat our emotions like smelly socks? What
   do we need to do about this tendency?

D. Look again at the bulleted scriptures at the end of the "Connection Is a Command" section of chapter 12. What is God telling His men about their need to get connected with others? Comment on the scriptures that seem most relevant to your own situation.

E. Review together the entire section in chapter 13 titled "Diversion Talks." Discuss the diversionary tactics used by Palmer, Alan, and Jack. How are these effective? Destructive? Which have you used in the past?

F. Later in chapter 13 you read the story about Chrissy's finding Kenny's journal/workbook. Can you understand Chrissy's reaction? What do you think of Kenny's response? How should a man respond?

Note: If you're following a twelve-week track,
save the rest of this lesson for the next session.
If you are on an eight-week track, keep going.

☑ EVERY MAN'S CHOICE
(Questions for Personal Reflection and Examination, Chapter 14)

📖 The mistake I see God's men making is attempting to reach new spiritual heights without some sort of guide to help them along. They leave base camp full of hope, ready to trek through life, but forgetting that they could go much farther—and higher—if they remembered to have a certain Guide come along: the Holy Spirit. 📖

     📖 Jesus knew that His leaderless followers might decide
to head for the hills after He was no longer physically with
them. That's why He took special care to inform them of the
coming transition, even though He knew the disciples would
only be able to absorb some of it intellectually—and almost
none of it emotionally. 📖

11. Think back on some specific times in your life when you could have
used a spiritual guide. Be honest: Were you truly listening to and
heeding the Holy Spirit's guidance during those times? These days, to
what extent do you consider the Holy Spirit your guide for climbing
the spiritual mountains of life?

12. Read John 14:15-18. If you had been one of the original disciples,
how well would you have understood what was going to happen in
the days ahead?

👟 EVERY MAN'S WALK

(Your Guide to Personal Application, Chapter 14)

     📖 Changes inspire fear. Changes create discomfort.
Changes require taking new risks. Changes also take us

to the next level. Learning to rely on the Holy Spirit may be new to you. But just get to know Him. You'll be *more* than fine. 📖

📖 The fact is we possess God's Spirit and have the clear instruction from God's Word on His role and how to work with Him.

Your next step as God's man is to understand the person of the Holy Spirit and get to know Him intimately. Then you can willingly partner with Him to reach new spiritual heights. 📖

13. Is learning to rely on the guidance of the Holy Spirit a big change for you? If so, what are your main concerns?

14. Get to know the Spirit! You'll find biblical information by reviewing the ten bulleted scriptures in the section subtitled "Transition and Trust: Taking the Next Step." Look up all the passages, and read them in their full context. Of all these verses, which are the most inspiring for you? Why?

15. The authors (and Scripture) convey the analogy between control by alcohol and control by the Spirit. When have you been under the control and influence of the Spirit? How well can you trust Him?

16. Read through the prayer at the end of chapter 14. If it expresses the desire of your heart right now, pray it to the Lord with a sincere heart.

17. What for you was the most meaningful concept or truth in this week's study? What action step(s) do you sense God is leading you to take in response?

How would you talk this over with God? Write your response here as a prayer to Him.

🗣 EVERY MAN'S TALK

(Constructive Questions for Group Discussion, Chapter 14)

Key Highlights from the Book to Read Aloud and Discuss

📖 I believe few men realize they can have a close partnership with the Holy Spirit—someone who will speak directly into their minds and walk with them every step of the way. In fact, if you let Him, He'll guide you to the top of any summit you want to climb.

But you've got to be ready to adjust. 📖

📖 A couple of disciples might have been scratching their heads, thinking, *Okay, a couple of minutes ago, He just said He had to go to prepare a place for us, and now He's saying He's not leaving. Another Counselor? Where's He going to live?* Jesus knew the nature of these plans would bring a shock to the system, so He reiterated it all a few minutes later [see John 16:7-8,13-15]. 📖

📖 Listen to what the Holy Spirit is ready to do in our lives right now. 📖

Discussion Questions for Chapter 14

An opening question: Which parts of chapter 14 were most helpful or encouraging to you? Why?

G. Has anyone in the group had experience with mountain climbing? Ask him about the importance of having a guide on an Everest-like expedition.

H. Together, review the story of Roger and Jason. Have you ever had to adjust to change like that? What happened? In what ways might learning to trust the Spirit be a similar kind of upsetting jolt?

I. Keeping the second quotation above in mind, ask someone in the group to read aloud John 16:7-8,13-15. Talk about how you would have reacted to these words of Jesus if you'd been one of His disciples at the time.

J. See the bulleted list of Bible passages in the section subtitled "Transition and Trust: Taking the Next Step." What is the most inspiring passage for you in this list? Why?

K. The authors contend that when we say yes to the Spirit, we are saying no to our sins. Do you agree? How can this work, in practical terms, in any man's daily life?

along for the ride?

This week's reading assignment:

chapters 15–17 in *Every Man, God's Man*

We are like the boxer who keeps getting knocked down but rises again to continue fighting. We are like the silver miner who straps on a helmet, descends into the mine shaft, and keeps chipping away at the ore until he emerges with something precious at the end of the day. Our spiritual journey keeps us getting up following knock-downs, keeps us showing up each morning at the silver mines. God's men are realistic and optimistic, taking the long view.

So, out of gratitude for what God has done in our lives, we endure. Out of devotion…we persist. Out of obedience, we hold on. Out of faith, we persevere.

—from chapter 16 in *Every Man, God's Man*

EVERY MAN'S TRUTH
(Your Personal Journey into God's Word)

Perseverance under pressure pleases God. What does this mean for you? That you will stick with God's way in the absence of an immediate result? That you will do God's will whether you feel like it or not? That you will serve your wife, for example, without resentment because it pleases God?

Surely you can add to the list, but none of it will be easy. So before you launch into this study, let the words of these scriptures permeate your heart and mind. They'll help you to keep on keeping on in the faith.

> Do you not know?
>> Have you not heard?
> The LORD is the everlasting God,
>> the Creator of the ends of the earth.
> He will not grow tired or weary,
>> and his understanding no one can fathom.
> He gives strength to the weary
>> and increases the power of the weak.
> Even youths grow tired and weary,
>> and young men stumble and fall;
> but those who hope in the LORD
>> will renew their strength.
> They will soar on wings like eagles;
>> they will run and not grow weary,
>> they will walk and not be faint. (Isaiah 40:28-31)

Not that I have already obtained all this, or have already been made perfect, but I press on to take hold of that for which Christ Jesus took hold of me. Brothers, I do not consider myself yet to have taken hold of it. But one thing I do: Forgetting what is behind and straining toward what is ahead, I press on toward the goal to win the prize for which God has called me heavenward in Christ Jesus. (Philippians 3:12-14)

Since we are surrounded by such a great cloud of witnesses, let us throw off everything that hinders and the sin that so easily entangles, and let us run with perseverance the race marked out for us. Let us fix our eyes on Jesus, the author and perfecter of our faith, who for the joy set before him endured the cross, scorning its shame, and sat down at the right hand of the throne of God. Consider him who endured such opposition from sinful men, so that you will not grow weary and lose heart.

In your struggle against sin, you have not yet resisted to the point of shedding your blood. And you have forgotten that word of encouragement that addresses you as sons:

> "My son, do not make light of the Lord's discipline,
>> and do not lose heart when he rebukes you,
> because the Lord disciplines those he loves,
>> and he punishes everyone he accepts as a son."

Endure hardship as discipline; God is treating you as sons. For what son is not disciplined by his father?...

Therefore, strengthen your feeble arms and weak knees. (Hebrews 12:1-7,12)

1. Think about a time when your strength was renewed for a kingdom task. How was God involved in your renewal?

2. Why was the apostle Paul not content to rest? What was the great prize he desired at the finish line of the race of faith?

3. How does it make you feel to know that you are surrounded by witnesses as you seek to grow in Christ?

4. What does it mean to you that Jesus is the author and perfecter of your faith?

☑ EVERY MAN'S CHOICE

(Questions for Personal Reflection and Examination, Chapter 15)

📖 Inside of every God's man there is a living, breathing vortex of supernatural power. Through prayer, our faith is placed in a powerful person and in His promises. Consider these... 📖

📖 We're afraid that too many men don't realize they can have an even *better* friend-to-friend relationship with Jesus

Christ. And it's not about putting in a lot of prayer time to make that happen—that would be misunderstanding the context and purpose of prayer. Instead, when God's man puts prayer into the realm of interacting with God, he talks to God not only when he's seeking relief or comfort but (more important) because God is an indispensable, intimate confidant. 📖

5. Read the first quotation above, then review the six scripture promises under the subheading "The Vortex" near the start of chapter 15. Which of these promises stands out most to you right now? Why?

6. Reflect on the level of intimacy you presently experience with God. Has your prayer life tended to be reserved for when you need help or guidance, or is it more of an ongoing interaction with Him?

 EVERY MAN'S **WALK**
(Your Guide to Personal Application, Chapter 15)

📖 God's man has a clear invitation to tap into God's personal storehouse of power and purpose. Just as the Colorado River was waiting for Arthur Davis to harness its power, God is waiting for us to tap into His awesome strength. The reality, for many of us, is that we are either clueless to the personal benefits of prayer or too hurried to slow down and get into the practice of prayer. We need to "think different," as the Apple computer ads say. 📖

📖 What drives you to pray and share your life with Jesus on a moment-by-moment basis? Is it relief or relationship? What moves God's man to seek the connection that can give him the Holy Spirit's comfort and guidance through prayer? It's what God's man and Jesus Christ have between them—a cross. It has made the relationship possible, and it's what compels our conversations to be continual. 📖

7. When it comes to prayer, what does "think different" mean to you? Identify at least three ways in which you could start *today* to slow down your daily routine.

8. Think about the cross of Jesus for a moment—and all that it means to you. Make a list of the rich blessings that flow from that cross. Spend some time in prayerful thanksgiving.

9. The authors say that, after a while, tapping into God should feel natural to us. Is this true for you? Why or why not?

10. In quietness, review what you have written and learned in this week's study. If further thoughts or prayer requests come to your mind and heart, you may want to write them here.

👥 EVERY MAN'S TALK
(Constructive Questions for Group Discussion, Chapter 15)

Key Highlights from the Book to Read Aloud and Discuss

📖 The numbers are so huge that we cannot fathom how much power those generators produce. Yet all of that incredible power is barely a drop in the bucket compared to the vast reservoir of the power readily available to God's man: the power of prayer. Check this out: "Now to him who is able to do immeasurably *more* than all we ask or imagine, according to his power that is at work within *us*." (Ephesians 3:20). 📖

📖 Minutes after Glenn wakes up, he gulps coffee as he shaves, hits the shower, and gets dressed. A few minutes later, he grabs his cell phone from the charger, tosses a PowerBar and a bottle of Evian water into his satchel, and he's out the door. As soon as he's on the tollway, he powers up the phone, plugs in his earpiece, and starts listening to messages that have already come in from the East Coast....

Glenn knows that his tendency is to wait mainly for tough situations before he goes to God in prayer. He realizes his prayer life could and should be better. But he can't seem to work regular conversation with his Creator into the flow of his normal day.

I wonder what God thinks about all this. Can you imagine a relationship with a friend who contacts you only when he needs a favor or to say he's sorry?

And while these settings absolutely call for and should involve prayer, the practice of prayer should not have starting or stopping points, appropriate and inappropriate settings, or even certain set times. Search the Scriptures for boundaries into which prayer must fit and you will find none. 📖

Discussion Questions for Chapter 15

An opening question: Which parts of chapter 15 were most helpful or encouraging to you? Why?

A. Go back to the beginning of chapter 15 and review all the information about the Hoover Dam. Why does it seem easier to know the power of a great energy-generating project than to recognize the power of prayer?

B. Together, read the six scriptural promises in the section subtitled "The Vortex." Have each man talk about which of these promises means the most to him—and why.

C. Who can relate to Glenn's hectic daily pace? What practical changes could Glenn make to strengthen his prayer connection with God?

D. Have someone read aloud the six verses near the end of chapter 15 regarding the time and place for prayer. Then discuss this statement: "For God's man, prayer is an *attitude* he adopts toward all situations and relationships in which he finds himself." Why should prayer be considered an attitude as well as an action?

E. How, practically speaking, can we take a prayerful attitude into every situation and relationship in our lives?

Note: If you're following a twelve-week track,
save the rest of this lesson for the next session.
If you are on an eight-week track, keep going.

☑ EVERY MAN'S CHOICE
(Questions for Personal Reflection and Examination, Chapters 16 and 17)

📖 Having seen God mold and shape the lives of men over the years, Steve and I often feel like Todd the boat driver: We've seen our share of spiritual beginners who are unable to stand up on their single water ski. Being a Christian may *look* fun and easy....

Thank God that His expectations are different from our own. Listen to the liberating voice speaking His mind on our spiritual journey as God's men… 📖

📖 Before the president leaves the White House, every detail must be considered, clear boundaries secured, and well-rehearsed plans put in motion. In this sense, the leader of the free world is not a free man. *He can't just do as he pleases.* 📖

11. In chapter 16 take a look at the three printed scriptures that follow the first quotation above. What is God's view of you as you attempt to stand tall on your spiritual journey?

12. Can any man do whatever he wants? Why not? What about you? (Think of a key Scripture verse that will back up your claim.)

📖 EVERY MAN'S WALK

(Your Guide to Personal Application, Chapters 16 and 17)

📖 God is not looking for perfection; He's looking for and rewarding perseverance. So listen up, God's man: The message here is, *Don't give up the pursuit.* Hang in there. Keep trying to stand up on one ski. Try again and again, because the reward is great. 📖

📖 As God's men, we, too, must have predetermined boundaries to help us fulfill our commitments to Christ. What does that mean? Think about it. 📖

13. What things help you to keep getting up after you fall down while striving for your spiritual goals?

14. What kinds of boundaries do you have in place to keep you away from sin? Make a list!

15. In chapter 17, under the final subheading, "No Lanes, No Medal," you'll find a list of bulleted suggestions for establishing your boundaries. Which of these would you like to add to your list?

16. What for you was the most meaningful concept or truth in this week's study? What do you believe God wants you to do in response?

How would you talk this over with God? Write your response here as a prayer to Him.

Every Man's TALK
(Constructive Questions for Group Discussion, Chapters 16 and 17)

Key Highlights from the Book to Read Aloud and Discuss

📖 Most men with the nerve to approach me at a conference haven't exactly been resting peacefully on the sundecks of life. They're in the midst of violent storms that are beating down on their lives. They are grappling to make sense of things. As conflicts rage inside and out, they're trying to navigate their way through their personal hurricanes. 📖

📖 It's easy to be God's man when life is on a roll, isn't it? But it's another thing to be faithful in thought, word, and deed when we're caught in the vortex of life's storms. But that's exactly when God's man steps up to meet the challenge with integrity. Our response both *tests and reveals* the true depth of our spiritual character. 📖

📖 For many men I work with, giving up a relationship, a habit, or a job that they know is inconsistent with God's plan is almost as difficult as cutting off a hand. But the high goal of God's man—knowing and serving Christ—is worth any sacrifice or perceived loss. The message is this: *We must be ruthless in removing sin from our lives.* To do this we have to choose, ahead of time, the direction we will take. To do so, God's man has to proactively draw firm boundary lines that will help him maintain victory in the key domains of his existence—much as Billy Graham and Josh McDowell inspired me to do. 📖

Discussion Questions for Chapters 16 and 17

An opening question: Which parts of chapters 16 and 17 were most helpful or encouraging to you? Why?

F. Start your group time by recalling Kenny's water skiing adventure. See if any of the men can share similar stories of trying, failing, and persevering.

G. Have you been "resting peacefully on the sundecks of life"? If you haven't, you're normal! Talk about your own personal hurricane(s) if you can.

H. In chapter 16, under the section subtitled "Through the Hurricane," you'll find a bulleted list of ways in which perseverance under pressure pleases God. Identify those you have experienced, share with your group the process you went through, and the results of your perseverance.

I. Go to the first three paragraphs of chapter 17, including the bulleted list of Josh McDowell's boundary rules. What do you think of these kinds of rules for God's men? Have you ever sensed that you needed to set up moral boundaries in advance? Why or why not?

J. What does it mean, in practical terms, to be ruthless in removing sin from our lives? What encouragement can you offer one another in this area?

K. Go through the bulleted examples of boundaries listed near the end of chapter 17. Talk about each one, sharing specific ideas of clear boundaries that will help you and your group members stay morally, spiritually, and sexually pure.

leave your baggage behind

This week's reading assignment:

chapters 18–19 in *Every Man, God's Man*

Practically speaking, if a man loves God and is doing everything we've presented in this book, but he's still in bondage to a particular hang-up or habit, that's a sign to us that there is still some unfinished business in need of God's healing touch. Past hurts motivate present behavior, and the man's relationships—including his connection to God—will be negatively influenced by those hurts until the root causes are discovered, acknowledged, and brought to Him.

And only the bravest of God's men go there. Why? Because it means examining some painful truths we would rather forget.

—from chapter 18 in *Every Man, God's Man*

EVERY MAN'S TRUTH

(Your Personal Journey into God's Word)

As you begin this final study, prayerfully consider the wounds you've experienced in your life. Think about the kinds of healing you've received so far and the types of healing you still need. Can God meet you at this point of need? Can He bring into your life healing and restoration? These are questions even the biblical authors were asking. Yet they continually proclaimed a God of love and goodness who cares for us and never leaves us. May these readings bless your heart as you continue the journey toward becoming God's man.

> How long, O LORD? Will you forget me forever?
>   How long will you hide your face from me?
> How long must I wrestle with my thoughts
>   and every day have sorrow in my heart?
>   How long will my enemy triumph over me?
>
> Look on me and answer, O LORD my God.
>   Give light to my eyes, or I will sleep in death;
> my enemy will say, "I have overcome him,"
>   and my foes will rejoice when I fall.
>
> But I trust in your unfailing love;
>   my heart rejoices in your salvation.
> I will sing to the LORD,
>   for he has been good to me. (Psalm 13:1-6)

To keep me from becoming conceited because of these surpassingly great revelations, there was given me a thorn in my flesh, a messenger of Satan, to torment me. Three times I pleaded with the Lord to take it away from me. But he said to me, "My grace is sufficient for you, for my power is made perfect in weakness." Therefore I will boast all the more gladly about my weaknesses, so that Christ's power may rest on me. That is why, for Christ's sake, I delight in weaknesses, in insults, in hardships, in persecutions, in difficulties. For when I am weak, then I am strong. (2 Corinthians 12:7-10)

1. Can you think of a time when you asked God "how long"? How long *was* it before He seemed to respond?

2. What does it say to you that the Lord let Paul's "thorn" stay in place?

3. Like Paul, perhaps you can think of a time when your weakness proved to be your greatest strength (when placed in God's hands). What do you remember thinking and feeling before you gave it to God? What did He teach you through the experience?

☑ EVERY MAN'S **CHOICE**
(Questions for Personal Reflection and Examination)

> 📖 Trevor fears failure because failure will mean rejection. Rejection is kryptonite for an approval addict. So to prevent failure in relationships, in raising kids, and in interacting with others, situations have to be controlled, predictable, and produce the desired outcomes....

After meeting hundreds of men just like Trevor in one-on-one relationships, we have reached these simple conclusions, which come straight out of the life experiences of these men (including ourselves)... 📖

📖 Becoming God's man hinges on what motivates us. And Scripture is clear regarding what we should place squarely at the center: God's man regards the unique and personal sacrifice of Jesus Christ as the single most powerful determinant of his choices—*in every domain of life.* 📖

4. Review Trevor's story at the beginning of chapter 18, then consider the authors' five conclusions about how life experiences shape men. Which of these are powerfully evident in your own life?

5. What motivates you toward spiritual growth? Are you sure?

👟 EVERY MAN'S WALK
(Your Guide to Personal Application)

📖 The fact is that legacies of abandonment, disapproval, divorce, or anger rob boys of the father blessing and predispose them to self-destructive tendencies as grown men:

- They create distance between us and God.
- They damage our relationships with people.
- They increase our vulnerability to the world, the flesh, and Satan.
- They draw us into disobedience to God's plan. 📖

📖 Dubbed the "Prince of Preachers" by his contemporaries, Charles H. Spurgeon approached moving people toward a courageous faith and spiritual integrity by getting them to take a long look at how Christ died for them. This would spur them to find, or regain, their spiritual impetus. What does recalling Christ's sacrifice do? Consider:

- It calls for a personal response.
- It renews our determination.
- It reshapes our relationships.
- It redirects our passions.
- It redefines our purpose. 📖

6. Take some time to analyze the impact of past wounds on your present actions. Where are the hurts still taking their toll?

7. Spend several minutes just meditating on Christ's sacrifice for you. What things are you moved to say to God in prayer?

8. At the end of the section subtitled "A Call to Courageous Faith" in chapter 19, the authors provide six bulleted questions regarding what it will take to become God's man. Answer each one prayerfully.

9. In quietness, review what you have written and learned in this week's study. If further thoughts or prayer requests come to your mind and heart, you may want to write them here.

10. What for you was the most meaningful concept or truth in this week's study? What do you believe God wants you to do in response?

How would you talk this over with God? Write your response here as a prayer to Him.

EVERY MAN'S TALK

(Constructive Questions for Group Discussion)

Key Highlights from the Book to Read Aloud and Discuss

  📖 A man will spend decades of his life trying to compensate for gaps in his relationship with his dad. Until healing occurs, attempts to compensate will draw him into destructive lifestyles, habits, addictions, and failed relationships. 📖

  📖 Regardless of our losses, our needs for intimacy, affirmation, and connection are met in our heavenly Father. No earthly pursuit, power, possession, or pleasure will suffice, and no medicine can heal a wound like the love and grace of God made known in the person of Christ. That is why Jesus, in the parable of the prodigal son, shocked His hearers by depicting the Father as eager to run to us so that He can embrace us upon our return home. 📖

Discussion Questions

An opening question: Which parts of chapter 18 and 19 were most helpful or encouraging to you? Why?

A. Begin your group time by focusing on the beginning of chapter 18, which details Trevor's story. What is your reaction to the idea that the father-son relationship is critical to the son's development into healthy manhood? Do you have any evidence of your own to back up your position?

B. According to the authors, how would addictions relate to the father-son relationship? to other problems?

C. Why can't an earthly pursuit heal our wounds? What have you tried so far? What is the better alternative?

D. What was, and is, so shocking about the prodigal son parable? What does it mean to you in your personal relationship with the heavenly Father?

E. Spend your remaining time on the section of chapter 19 called "Make the Choice of Choices" and on to the end of the book. Talk about the historic Packers game, Bart Starr, and the spiritual principles that Kenny draws from that monumental game. What principles have the most impact for you?

F. Since this is your final session together, take a moment to reflect on what you've studied and discussed during the previous weeks. Ask each man to comment on one or more of these questions:

- What can you thank God for as a result of this study?

- What do you sense God most wants you to understand now about this topic?

- In what specific ways do you believe He wants you now to more fully trust and obey Him?

- Shall we make plans to meet again for fellowship—or to start a new study group in the future?

don't keep it to yourself

If you've just completed the *Every Man, God's Man Workbook* on your own, and you found it to be a helpful and valuable experience, we encourage you to consider organizing a group of men and helping lead them through the book and workbook together.

You'll find more information about starting such a group in the section titled "Questions You May Have About This Workbook."

about the authors

Stephen Arterburn is coauthor of the best-selling Every Man series. He is founder and chairman of New Life Clinics, host of the daily "New Life Live!" national radio program, creator of the Women of Faith Conferences, a nationally known speaker and licensed minister, and the author of more than forty books. He lives with his family in Laguna Beach, California. Steve can be reached by e-mail at sarterburn@newlife.com.

Kenny Luck is president and founder of Every Man Ministries. He is division leader for men's small groups and a member of the teaching staff of Saddleback Valley Community Church in Lake Forest, California. He and his wife, Chrissy, have three children and reside in Rancho Santa Margarita, California. Kenny can be reached by e-mail at everymanministry@aol.com.

Mike Yorkey is the author, coauthor, or general editor of more than thirty books, including all the books in the Every Man series. He and his wife, Nicole, are the parents of two college-age children and live in Encinitas, California.

start a bible study
and connect with others
who want to be God's man.

If you enjoyed the *Every Man, God's Man Workbook,* you'll love the Every Man Bible Studies, designed to help you discover, own, and build on convictions grounded in God's word.

being God's man...
in leading a family

Real Men. Real Life. Powerful Truth.

Stephen Arterburn
Kenny Luck & Todd Wendorff

being God's man...
in tough times

Real Men. Real Life. Powerful Truth.

Stephen Arterburn
Kenny Luck & Todd Wendorff

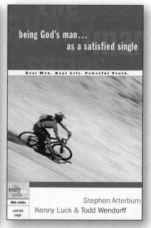

being God's man...
as a satisfied single

Real Men. Real Life. Powerful Truth.

Stephen Arterburn
Kenny Luck & Todd Wendorff

being God's man...
in the search for success

Real Men. Real Life. Powerful Truth.

Stephen Arterburn
Kenny Luck & Todd Wendorff

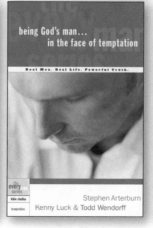

being God's man...
in the face of temptation

Real Men. Real Life. Powerful Truth.

Stephen Arterburn
Kenny Luck & Todd Wendorff

being God's man...
by pursuing friendships

Real Men. Real Life. Powerful Truth.

Stephen Arterburn
Kenny Luck & Todd Wendorff

WATERBROOK PRESS
www.waterbrookpress.com

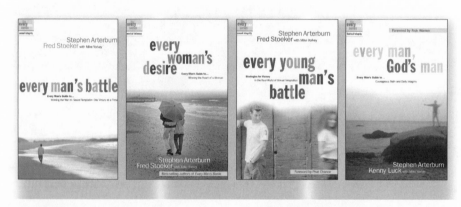